BASIC KNOWLEDGE IN CIVIL ENGINEERING

(NR)-1

V.NARASIMHA

Basic knowledge in civil engineering

2019

Revised 2020

VAVILALA NARASIMHA

DIPLOMA, B.TECH IN CIVIL ENGINEERING

(GOVT POLYTECHNIC ST. GHANPUR, WARANGAL)

Preface

The main aim of writing this book is to provide the basic knowledge in civil engineering for the students by analyzing pictures and diagrams to get practical knowledge.

This book was written by referring many other civil engineering books

It is essential to a civil engineer to have a minimum basic knowledge in civil engineering Such as unit conversions, sizes of components of building, building bye laws, history of civil engineering, reinforcement, technical terms, estimation of bricks for a wall etc.

This book is written in simple, easily understandable way.

I express sincere thanks to my parents and my friends

I hope that this book will prove immensely useful for civil engineering students.

Dedicated to my lecturers

Contents

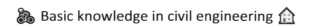 Basic knowledge in civil engineering

INTRODUCTION

Civil engineering: A branch of engineering concerned with planning, designing and construction of roads, buildings, bridges, dams, canals, sewers, pipe lines etc.

★ Engineer who design, plan, construct, maintain and operate infrastructures is called civil engineer.

Building: A building is a structure consist of foundation, roof, walls etc. and used for many purposes such as

- Shelter to human
- Accommodation purpose
- Protect from heavy rain, sun heat etc.

Types of buildings

1. Residential: family private dwelling, lodge, rooms, dormitories, apartments, hotels.

2. Institutional: Hospitals, homes for aged, mental hospitals, dharmshala, prisons, nursing homes.

3. Educational: schools, colleges etc.

4. Business: Offices, banks, computer installations etc.

5. Hazardous: Consisting of explosive material, highly flammable.

6. Industrial: Power plants, refineries, gas plants, dairy products, saw mills etc.

7. Assembly: Assembly halls, theatres, dance halls, auditoria, places of worship, museums etc.

8. Mercantile: shops, markets, underground shopping centres.

9.storage: store houses, garages, storing of goods.

1. World's greatest structures

1. World's longest sea bridge

In China Zhuhai Macau bridge connecting Hong Kong to Chinese city.

The bridge is about 55km long.

Chinese President xi jinping has officially opened

that bridge in 2018. Period of construction is 9years.

2. World's tallest statue: " statue of unity "

Sardhar vallabhai patel statue Located in India in Gujarat inaugurated by

Prime minister of India Narendra modi in 31st October 2018.

Height of the statue is 182 metres located on Narmada river It was built by Larsen & toubro.

3. World's tallest structure

Burj Khalifa in Dubai (UAE) about 829.8 metres

Tallest structure in world

 Basic knowledge in civil engineering 🏠

4. World's deepest laboratory

JINPING underground laboratory in China

About 7900 feet deep structure.

2. Unit conversions

Feet is represented by (') and inch is represented by (")

1. One metre = 3.28' or 3'3.375"

2. One feet = 0.3048 metres

3. 1 inch = 2.54 centimetres.

4. 1kg = 2.20 pounds.

5. 1pound = 0.45 kg.

6. 1 yard = 0.91 metres.

7. 1 yard = 3'.

8. 1metre = 1.09 yards.

9. 1mile = 1.609 km.

10. One km = 0.62 miles.

11. One kg = 0.001 tonnes.

12. One m^3 = 1000 litre

13. One quintal = 100 kg

14. 1 feet square = 0.0929 m^2

15. 1acre = 4046.85 m^2

= 43560 sq. ft

= 40 gunta (1gunta=121sq.yards)

= 4840 sq. yards.

16. 1feet = 0.33 yards.

17. 1 acre = 0.4046 hectares.

18. 1 hectare = 10,000 sq. metres

= 2.47 acres

19. 1 kg. f = 9.81 N

20. Density of water = 1000 kg/m^3.

21. Sp. weight of water = 9810 N/m^3

22. 1 psi = 703.069 kg/m^2

= 6894.75 pascal

(Psi = pound per square inch).

23. 1psi = 144psf

(Psf = pound per square foot)

24. Pound is denoted by (lb)

25. 1 U.S gallon = 3.785 litres

26. 1°centigrade = 33.8°F

27. 1°farenheit = -17.22° Celsius

28. 1kelvin = -272.15° Celsius

 Basic knowledge in civil engineering 🏠

3.History of civil engineering

Engineering is the prominent one to survive in this world.

Earliest practice of civil engineering may be started between 4000 - 2000 BC in ancient Egypt.

During Indus Valley civilization when human started creating a need for construction of shelter during this time transportation has started and lead to development of wheel and sailing.

1. Pyramids of Egypt constructed between (2700 - 2500 BC)

2. Qanat water management around (3000 BC).

It is an underground sloping

channel or tunnel.

It is used for the purpose

Of irrigation Facilities and other purposes

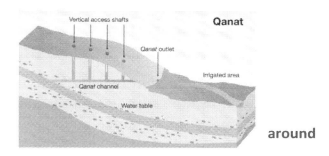

3. Parthenon by Iktinos in ancient Greece (447 - 438 BC) around

Ictinus is an architect

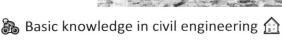 Basic knowledge in civil engineering 🏠

4. Appian way by Roman engineers (312 BC)

Appian way is ancient road way.

5. Great wall of China by general MENG TIEN around (220 BC)

Romans developed civil structures include aqueduct, bridges, harbours, dams, roads.

Aqueduct built in 19BC

First self-proclaimed civil engineer was John Smeaton.

Term civil engineering was coined by him

John Smeaton is the father of civil engineering

He born in England (18 June 1724) and died in (28 oct1792)

He constructed bridges, canals and light house

He is a British civil engineer.

Eddy stone light house (49m height) in England was constructed by him.

 Basic knowledge in civil engineering

4.How $D^2/162.2$ and how to calculate weight of steel bar.

Density = mass/volume

Mass = volume × density

Density of steel = 7850kg/m^3, volume = π/4 × D^2× length

Mass of steel for 1m^3 or 1000mm^3 = π/4 × D^2 × 1000 × 7850/1000^3

(considering in millimetres, because steel bar is in mm)   = π/4 × D^2 × 1000 × 7850×10^{-9}

= D^2× 6.165×10^{-3}

= D^2/162.2

So, unit weight of steel for 1metre = D^2/162.2

D = diameter of bar in mm

For 10mm diameter bar, weight of bar for 1metre = 10^2/162.2

= 0.6165 kg/m

Generally, bar length is 12 metres.

5. GRADES OF CONCRETE

Grade in N/mm² and M - mix

For nominal mix

1. M5 = 1:5:10 (1-part cement, 5 parts fine aggregate, 10 parts coarse aggregate)

2. M7.5 = 1:4:8

3. M10 = 1:3:5

4. M15 = 1:2:4

5. M20 = 1:1.5:3

6. M25 = 1:1:2

6. SIZES OF DRAWING SHEETS

A0	841 × 1189
A1	594 × 841
A2	420 × 594
A3	297 × 420
A4	210 × 297
A5	148 × 210

7.SIZES OF BUILDING COMPONENTS

1. Height of storey

For Office = 3.9 metres (12.79 feet's).

For Residential = 3.1 metres (10.17 feet's).

And should not be less than 2.75 metres.

2. Door sizes

For residential buildings

a) Exterior = 1.0 × 2.0 m to 1.1 × 2.0 m

b) Interior = 0.9 × 2.0 m to 1.0 × 2.0 m

Bath rooms and water closets = 0.7 × 2.0 m to 0.8 × 2.0 m

For public buildings

a) 1.2 × 2.0 m
b) 1.2 × 2.1 m
c) 1.2 × 2.25 m

Garages = 2.25 × 2.25 m to 2.40 × 2.25 m

3. Window sizes

a) 1.5 × 1.2 m
b) 1.2 × 1.25 m
c) 1.0 × 1.2 m

4. Wall thickness

a) 230 mm (or) 9 inches {external wall}

b) 125 mm (or) 5 inches. {Internal wall}

5. Height of parapet wall

= not less than 1m and not greater than 1.5m.

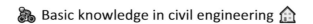 Basic knowledge in civil engineering 🏠

8. COVER

➤ Generally, cover

For slabs - 20mm

For beams - 25mm

For columns - 40mm

For footings - 50mm

9. WHAT IS PLAN AND TYPES

Plan: Drawing or a diagram drawn on a plane to represent something and to execute it.

Example: plan of a building

1) Key plan: A plan drawn to show boundary and location of site with respect of neighbouring land marks. Plan having scale not less than 1: 10000

2) Site plan: site plan consists of a) land belonging to owner

   b) Names of street on which building is proposed

   c) All adjacent streets, distance from electrical line to building

   d) width of streets, placement of trees etc.

Site plan is drawn to a scale of 1:100 for plots up to 500 sq.mt. in size and scale of 1: 500 for plots above 500 sq.mt. in size

3) Building plan: It consists of a) floor plans of all floors

   b) staircases, ramps, lift ways, exit ways, W.C, sink, bath etc.

   c) giving indications of north point

   d) location of firefighting equipment

   e) vehicular parking spaces

Building plan is drawn to a scale of 1:50 for plots up to 250 sq.mt. and 1:100 for plots above 250 sq.mt.

4. Services plan: plans, elevations, sections of private water supply, sewage disposal system for scale not less than 1: 100

10. AAC BLOCKS

AAC stands for autoclave aerated concrete blocks

These blocks are light in weight

Composition of AAC blocks

1. Cement

2. Water

3. Fly ash or sand (silica rich material)

4. Lime stone powder

5. Aluminium powder/paste

6. Gypsum

   ❖ Size of block is 600 × 200 × 100 to 300 mm

   ❖ Density of block is 550 - 650 kg/cu.metre.

Autoclave: strong heated container used for heating at high temperature and pressure.

Nowadays these types of blocks are used in building construction

11. S.B.C OF SOIL

As per IS 6403: 1981

Safe bearing capacity: The loading that carry the soil without shear failure of soil is called **S.B.C**

Ultimate bearing capacity: Which causes shear failure

Allowable bearing capacity: The loading that doesn't cause settlement of soil

Types of tests:

Ultimate bearing capacity is done by shear failure test

1) plate load test (IS 1888 - 1982)

2) Determination of shear strength by (IS: 2720 part 13 1986)

3) static cone penetration test (IS 4968 part 3 - 1976)

12. GENERAL KNOWLEDGE

1) surface area of earth = 510 million sq.km.

   land surface = 29.08%

   water surface = 70.92%

   Continents = 7 and oceans = 5

2) largest country is Russia (17075200 sq.km.)

   Smallest country is Vatican City (0.44 sq.km)

   India is the seventh largest country in the world

3) Period of revolution of earth around sun is 360days 5hrs 48min 45.51seconds.

   Rotation of earth on its own axis is 23hrs 56min 4.09sec.

4) Radius of earth = 6371km.

   Diameter of earth at equator = 12754 km.

   Diameter of earth at poles = 12714 km.

5) longest river in the world is Nile river about 6650 km.

   largest lake in the world is Caspian Sea about 1199 km.

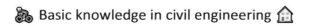

13. CARRIAGE WAY

Carriage way is defined as the way along which traffic passes. It is also called as width of pavement.

➢ For single lane road width is 3.75 metres

➢ For two lane road width is 7.0 metres (each - 3.5m)

➢ For multi lane road, each lane is 3.5 metres.

14. TRAFFIC SIGNS

1) Regulatory (or) mandatory signs: These signs are kept in circular shape of 600mm diameter at 2.8m. from ground level.

It consists of No parking, No horn, speed limit 20,

Dead slow, No turn and No overtaking

2) Warning (or) cautionary signs: These signs are in triangular plate of 450mm width

Examples: level crossing, school,

Rough road,

turns i.e. right, left, U- turn etc.

3) Informatory (or) guiding signs: For giving particular information about route

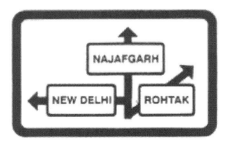

 Basic knowledge in civil engineering 🏠

15. PLAN OF ROW TYPE BUILDING

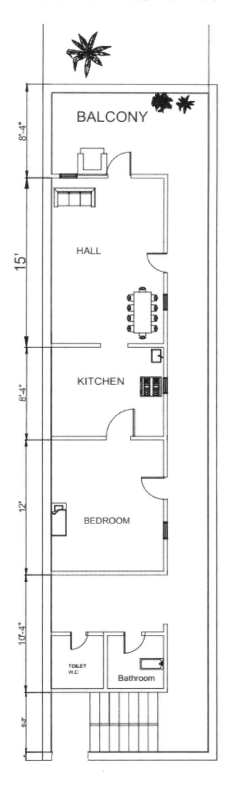

PLAN

16.CEMENT

Cement was invented by Joseph aspdin and patented in the year 1824 in England.

First, cement was made at limestone quarry in England near Portland city and it was named as Portland cement

Limestone is the main constituent in manufacturing of cement

Cement is a binding Material which is obtained by burning calcareous, siliceous & argillaceous materials together at high temperature in definite proportions and grinding resultant clinker to fine powder.

<u>Composition of Portland cement:</u>

Lime - 60 to 67%

Silica - 18 to 25%

Alumina - 5 to 9%

Iron oxide - 0.5 to 6%

Magnesium oxide - 0.1 to 4%

Sulphur trioxide - 1 to 3%

Soda or potash - 0.5 to 1.3%

Insoluble residues - 0.5%

Gypsum - 1 to 3%

Opc cement having three grades such as 53 grade, 43 grade, 33 grades.

Portland pozzolana cement is having opc plus fly ash to improve properties

 Basic knowledge in civil engineering

17. AGGREGATE

Aggregate is a material used in construction. Aggregates are two types they are 1) fine aggregate 2) coarse aggregate.

❖ The aggregate which pass through 4.75mm IS sieve and retained on 75 microns IS sieve is called fine aggregate. examples: sand, robo sand (crushed stone powder), fine aggregate minimum size is 0.075mm and maximum size is 4.75mm.

Sand

Robo sand

❖ The aggregate which pass through 75mm IS sieve and retained on 4.75mm IS sieve is called as coarse aggregate. examples: crushed stone, trap rock, dark coloured igneous rocks such as basalt, gabbro.

Kankar is the most common rock used as coarse aggregate in construction

Crushed stone

➢ *Sand is used for crack arrester and shrinkage reducer in mortar.*
➢ *Coarse aggregate is for strength and durability.*

18. BRICKS

➢ Bricks are made of clay, sand and small amount of lime **to unite particles during burning**

➢ Bricks are made during pre-pottery Neolithic period some oldest examples of brick were first found in Mesopotamia

➢ Many archaeological excavations made much information about brick and bricks are made by hand moulding in olden days

➢ The standard brick size as per Bureau of Indian standard is 19×9×9 cm.

➢ Bricks having high fire resistance up to 1220°c

➢ Normal red clay brick used in constructions size is 21×10×6.5 cm and other size also available depending upon manufacturer

19. RAILWAY GAUGES AND RAILS

Railway gauge: The clear distance between two inner faces of rails near their heads is known as gauge.

Types of gauges

1) Broad gauge - 1.676m

2) Metre gauge - 1m

3) Narrow gauge - 0.762m

4) Light gauge - 0.61m.

World standard gauge is 1.435 m. Indian standard gauge is broad gauge.

Rails: Rails are considered as steel girders used to carry loads and distribute to sleepers. From sleepers to ballast.

Types of rails: 1) Double headed rail   2) Bull headed rail   3) Flat footed rail.

➤ About 90% of world using flat footed rails.

➤ These rails were invented by "Charles vignoles" so, it is also known as VIGNOLES RAILS.

20. SPECIFIC GRAVITY

Specific gravity is the ratio of specific weight of substance to specific weight of water

Sp.gr = density of substance /density of water.

= Sp. weight of substance /sp. weight of water.

Specific gravity has no units it is dimensionless.

Specific gravity for different materials.

1) water(pure) = 1.0

2) sea water = 1.025

3) mercury = 13.6

4) kerosene = 0.82

5) milk = 1.035

6) wood = 0.701

7) coconut oil = 0.927

8) blood = 1.06

9) alcohol = 1.01

10) Diesel = 0.82 - 0.88

11) petrol = 0.739

21. MASS AND WEIGHT

Density = Mass/volume

Mass = Density × volume. Density in kg/m^3

Mass is expressed in kilogram and volume in cubic. Metre

Mass doesn't change from place to place but weight changes from place to place because acceleration due to gravity is different at equator and poles

Weight = mass × acceleration due to gravity so, weight in N or kg. force

Standard acceleration due to gravity on earth is 9.8 m/s^2

1kg = 9.81N so, specific weight of water is 9810 kg/m^3

Mass density of water = 1000 kg/m^3

Newton in kg × m/s^2

F = ma (mass × acceleration)

1kg = 9.81 kg × m/s^2

1kg = 9.81 N

22. BRIEF INFORMATION ABOUT STEEL

Iron: Iron is an element in the earth with atomic number is 26

Steel: steel is an alloy which is a mixture of iron and carbon and steel is having high tensile strength so it is used as reinforcement in concrete

Stainless steel: It is a mixture of steel and chromium. It is durable and doesn't undergo corrosion. It is corrosion resistance

Uses: Trusses, fixtures & fasteners in building units, bridges etc.

Mild steel: It is a type of steel having low carbon content and it is more ductile carbon content about 0.05 - 0.25%. It is not brittle and also called low carbon steel or plain carbon steel having low tensile strength

Having yield strength of 250 N/mm^2, better weldability and bent easily

These bars used as reinforcement in concrete till 1960

Uses: grills for windows, gates, machinery parts etc.

HYSD bars: High yield strength deformed bars are made by modifying mild steel by twisting steel rods after casting this cause flaws in bars. These are made by both cold and hot working process.

CTD bars: These are also called Tor steel. CTD means cold twisted deformed bars

➢ For manufacturing of CTD bars mild steel is subjected to hot rolling and twisted in cold condition and stretched. It is having strength 60% than mild steel

➢ These bars have yield strength of 415 N/mm^2 called as fe- 415 steel
➢ Welded joints are weak

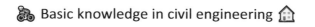
Basic knowledge in civil engineering

➢ Cracks appear on outer surface of CTD bars they loss strength on temperature.

CTD bars

TMT bars: These bars are not twisted but it involves rapid quenching of hot bars through a series of water jets this makes bar surface harden at top.

➢ These bars called as thermo mechanically treated bars.

➢ Having yield strength of 500 and 550 N/mm^2 named as fe- 500 and fe- 550.

➢ These bars are made by scraps and recycled metal.

➢ These bars having ribs on their surface for proper bond with concrete.

➢ They are having more tensile strength, ductility and some resistance to corrosion.

➢ They are started in India during 1980-1985.

R.C.C.

R.C.C was invented by Joseph monier and patented in 1867. He was a French gardener

23. TRUSS AND TYPES

Truss is defined as a framed structure composed of members connected to each other at their ends forming triangles.

> Uses:
> ➢ For very large spans to make structure economical
> ➢ At places where high rainfall to avoid roof drainage problems

Types:

1) King post truss

2) Queen post truss

3) Mansard roof truss

4) Fan truss

5) North light roof truss

6) Pratt truss

7) Howe truss

24. LOADS AND ITS CALCULATIONS

Loads that are calculated in designing a structure are

Dead load, live load, wind load, seismic load, erection load, snow load

Dead load: It is self-weight of structure. Density for different materials is given below

- For plain cement concrete - 24 KN/m^3

- For R.C.C - 25 KN/m^3 **Dead load calculation:**

- Brick - 19 KN/m^3 = volume × density

- Stone - 24 KN/m^3

- Wood - 8 KN/m^3

- Steel - 78.5 KN/m^3

Live load: It is the load that acting on structure it changes from time to time such as people occupying floor, furniture and machineries

Live load and erection load are calculated by IS: 875 part 2 - 1987

Wind load: The load act on structure due to wind

It is calculated by IS: 875 part 3 - 1987

Design Wind pressure = 0.6 Vz^2

Design wind velocity (Vz) = k1×k2×k3 × Vb

k1 = Risk coefficient (general buildings, important buildings, sheds etc.)

k2 = coefficient based on terrain, height and structure size

k3 = Topography factor (sloping ground, flat ground)

Vb = basic wind speed in m/s depending upon areas such as for Delhi - 47m/s, Hyderabad - 44m/s

Earth quake forces: earth quake forces depending upon region. For India it is design by IS: 1893 part 1- 2002

 Basic knowledge in civil engineering 🏠

25. SOME TERMS USED IN BUILDINGS

Porch: The extension of floor on front or back of entrance of building and covered by roof extending from main structure  is called porch.

Portico: It is a type of porch supported by rectangular or circular arrangement of columns.

Generally, height of portico is 2.1m

Verandah: The area, open at least one side and provided with roofed platform along outside of house its level with ground floor and extends across both front and sides of structure.

Balcony: platform on outside of building enclosed by walls or balusters and rails supported by beams and columns, having access from upper storey window or door, to serve sit out place

Corridor: It is a narrow hall or passage to all rooms.

Lobby: It is entrance or reception area.

Lane: Narrow or well-defined passage track, channel or a course.

Generally, it is used for expressing road such as single lane, two lane, four lanes etc.

Canopy: It is an overhead roof structure that has open sides to provide shelter from sun, rain and its height is not less than 2.3m from ground level.

canopy

Loggia: The room serve as corridor with more open sides as a series of arches supported by columns. Generally, one side is open to garden.

Patio: It is outdoor area used for dining recreation.

Basic knowledge in civil engineering

26. TERMS IN SOIL MECHANICS

Compaction: Removal of air voids from soil by applying loads

Consolidation: Removal of water voids from soil by application of loads

Machinery and tools: Needle vibrators, external vibrators, rollers, tamping rod etc.

Thixotropy: The property of soil of strength loose to strength gain is called thixotropy

The term soil mechanics was coined by Karl terzaghi

Residual soil: obtained by weathering of rocks

Laterite soil: It is in red colour due to iron oxide and very poor lime content

Black cotton soil: Having property of swelling and shrinkage due to change in moisture content.

Alluvial soil: Transported by running water ex: silt, clay, gravel.

Aeolian soil: Transported by wind ex: loess

Lacustrine soil: deposited in lakes

Glacier drift: Transported from glaciers

27. How 1Mpa is N/mm²

1 pascal = N/m²

   = 10^{-6} N/mm²

Mega = 10^6

So, 1 Mega pascal = $10^6 \times 10^{-6}$ N/mm²

   = N/mm²

28. FLYOVER, BRIDGE, CULVERT

Flyover: The name itself suggest that you are flying over traffic zone

It is built to join two or more points which are separated by an accessible route and also facilitates traffic in faster mode

It is only for road vehicles such as cars, buses etc.

Bridge: It is built to connect two points separated by a river, sea, valley etc.

It is used for Trains, cars, buses etc.

Bridge span is more than 6 meters

Culvert: structure that allows water to flow under road from one side to other side is called culvert

> Span of Culvert is not greater than 6 meters

🚲 Basic knowledge in civil engineering 🏠

29. FASTENERS

Fastener: It is a mechanical device that joins or affixes two or more objects.

Rivet: It is a permanent mechanical fastener consist of smooth cylindrical shaft with head on one end and tail on opposite end

It is placed in a punched or drilled hole

They won't loosen when subjected to vibration

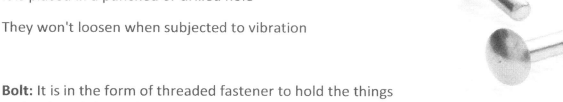

Bolt: It is in the form of threaded fastener to hold the things and it doesn't have sharp pointed end

Nut: It is a small metal having hole with threaded surface inside to fasten the parts together securely.

Bolt is inserted in nut to hold objects together

Screw: It is a sharp pointed metal with helical threaded surface around it and used to join different things

Nail: It is a thin body having sharp end point and doesn't have threaded structure

It is used for joining wood and similar materials

30. CELLAR, GODOWN, VAULT, CRYPT, CHAPEL

Cellar: It is storage space or room below ground level in house for storing things such as car parking

It is partly or wholly below ground level

Vault: It is a roof in the form of arch and series of arches

Godown: It is a place used to store raw material or goods. It is a warehouse.

Crypt: It is an underground place used as chapel or burial place

Chapel: A small building or room used for Christian worship in school, prison, hospital

31. PIER, PILE, CAISSON

Pier: structure resisting on piles or pillars projecting from shore to sea

❖ Shore means is edge of sea

And also, the structure which support the bridge and
distribute load to foundation is called
pier.

Pile: It is a timber, steel or concrete member which is driven into ground to support a structure and Bridge piers are supported on piles. These are used in loose soil foundation.

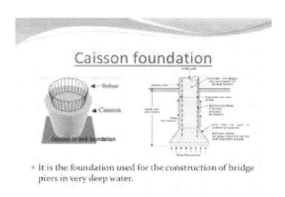

Caisson: It is a watertight structure used for construction

In this, by auguring deep hole into ground and fill it with RCC

It is a hollow structure used in underwater construction work.

Caisson foundation

* It is the foundation used for the construction of bridge piers in very deep water.

32. TOOLS   USED IN

  Basic knowledge in civil engineering

CONSTRUCTION WORK

Trowel: It is a small handheld tool with flat pointed blade used for spreading mortar.

Hoe: It is a tool with broad blade used for mixing concrete and used for digging other materials such as coal, earth etc. And it is also used for moving coal, snow etc. to certain place

Spade: It is a tool with sharp rectangular edge and used for digging or cutting earth

Screed: It is used for levelling concrete layer on slabs and it removes humps & hollows and give a uniform surface

Float: It is a small hand tool used for finishing concrete surface by making it smooth and removing irregularities

 Basic knowledge in civil engineering 🏠

Wheel barrow: It is an equipment having single wheel at front and supported on legs and having handles for carrying concrete in work

Steel square: It is used to measure right angle accurately in work

Hack - saw: It is used for cutting materials like wood, plastic etc.

Plumb - Bob: It is used as vertical reference line and it is used in construction

It is used in surveying operations

Glove: It is used as protective material for hands

 Basic knowledge in civil engineering 🏠

33. REVETMENT, RIPRAP, STONE PITCHING

Revetment: Revetments are sloping structures placed on banks of river in such a way to absorb energy of incoming water

If velocity increases under bridges it is necessary to provide revetment at bank and bottom of river

> ➤ Stone pitching is used on steep slopes
>
> ➤ Bank: It is a land alongside or sloping down to a river or lake

Stone pitching: In this, stones are placed

after dressed by pitched chisel.

Rip rap: A loose stone used to form a foundation for break water or other structure

Embankment: It is a wall or bank of earth or stone built to prevent flooding an area

34. DAM, COFFERDAM, RESERVOIR, SPILLWAY, SLUICE

Dam: It is a huge barrier constructed across the river or lake to store the water and utilize for many purposes

Coffer dam: It is a temporary structure constructed to enclose an area in water bodies and pump out the water from that area.

It is used to keep out water in constructing a bridge

Reservoir: It is an artificial lake used as source of water supply

It is the area developed by water body due to construction of dam

Spillway: It is to provide a controlled release of flows

 Basic knowledge in civil engineering

of water from dam. It is the portion over the water is flowed after gates opened.

Sluice: It is provided at bottom of dam for excluding silt in water

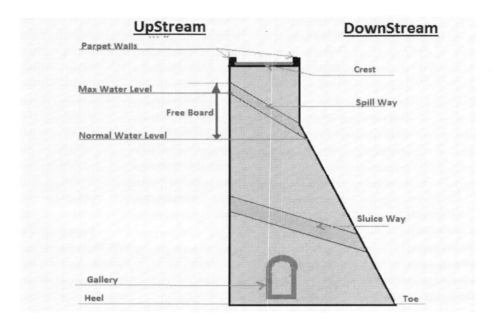

Abutment: The structure used to support the lateral pressure of span at ends of bridge and in culverts. It also resists lateral earth pressure.

🚲 Basic knowledge in civil engineering 🏠

35. BRICK ESTIMATION

Take the dimensions of the brick which is using in the work

For suppose a brick of size - 220×95×75 mm (without mortar thickness)

By including mortar thickness, the size of brick is 230×105×85 mm (considering thickness of mortar is 10mm)

No. Of bricks required for $1m^3$ = 0.23×0.105×0.085

$$= 2.05×10^{-3} \text{ cubic. Meter}$$

$$\text{For } 1m^3 = 1/2.05×10^{-3}$$

$$= 488 \text{ bricks}$$

C.C Beds.

Half brick wall.

For a half brick wall of height is 3m and width is 4m and take thickness of wall as 0.105m

Then volume of wall = 4×3×0.105 = $1.26m^3$

In a wall there are cement concrete beds

Consider there are 3 c.c beds of 100mm depth then volume of c.c beds is

$$= 4×0.1×0.105 = 0.042m^3$$

For 3 beds = 3×0.042 = $0.126m^3$

Deduct the c.c beds volume from wall = 1.26 - 0.126= $1.134m^3$

Total Number of bricks required for wall = 488×1.134

$$= 554 \text{ bricks.}$$

 Basic knowledge in civil engineering 🏠

36. CYCLONE, TSUNAMI, DISASTER, EARTHQUAKE

Cyclone: It is a meteorological phenomenon in which a large-scale air mass that rotates around a strong centre of low barometric pressure and air rises, the moisture in air form clouds and resulting a heavy storm

Meteorology: science that deals with atmosphere

Hurricane: A tropical cyclone having wind more than 74 miles/hour.

Storm: A violent disturbance of atmosphere with strong winds and usually rain, thunders, lightening, tornadoes is called storm

Tornado: The rotating winds having funnel shaped with a huge air mass that is contact with both earth and clouds resulting a great damage to life and property

Tsunami: Tsunami or a tidal wave. A series of waves in water body caused due to earthquake or other disturbance.

Biggest tsunami is at a height of 100 feet

Disaster: A sudden accident or natural catastrophe causes great damage

It is caused naturally and man - made

Catastrophe: great sudden damage

Earthquake: A sudden violent shaking of ground causing great destruction due to tectonic movements

37. STIRRUPS AND LATERAL TIES

Stirrup: Stirrups are installed around the reinforcement in beams to resist against shear in the structural member

Stirrups are used in beams

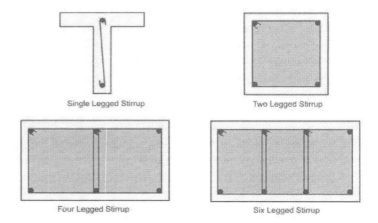

Single Legged Stirrup

Two Legged Stirrup

Four Legged Stirrup

Six Legged Stirrup

Lateral ties: These are used to hold the longitudinal reinforcement in columns and prevent the longitudinal reinforcement from buckling

Lateral ties are used in columns

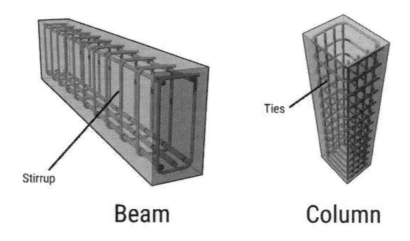

Stirrup

Beam

Ties

Column

38. SLABS AND ITS TYPES

Slab: slab is a structural member used as roof covering and floor covering

slab transfer the load to beam and from beam to column load is distributed. Some slabs are laid directly over columns

Main reinforcement is used to resist bending and distribution reinforcement is provided to hold main reinforcement and to resist against cracks due to shrinkage stresses

Types of slabs:

1) one-way slab: slab supported on two opposite edges and whose ratio of longer Span to shorter span is > 2 is called as one-way slab

Slab bends in one direction only so main reinforcement is provided in one direction

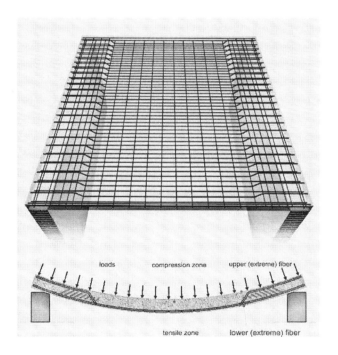

2) Two-way slab: This type of slab is supported on four edges and ratio of longer span to shorter span is < or = 2 then it is called two-way slab

To resist two way bending main reinforcement is provided in two directions

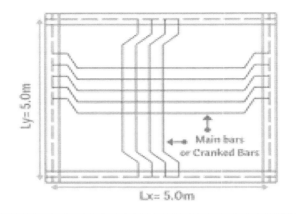

$\frac{Ly}{Lx} = \frac{5}{5} = 1$ which is < 2

Hence Two way slab is adopted

Main bars or Cranked Bars

Ly= 5.0m

Lx= 5.0m

Two Way Slab

3) Flat slab: Slab supported directly on columns without beams is called flat slab

Flat slab is provided with drops and head on columns

39. HYDRO ELECTRIC POWER PLANT

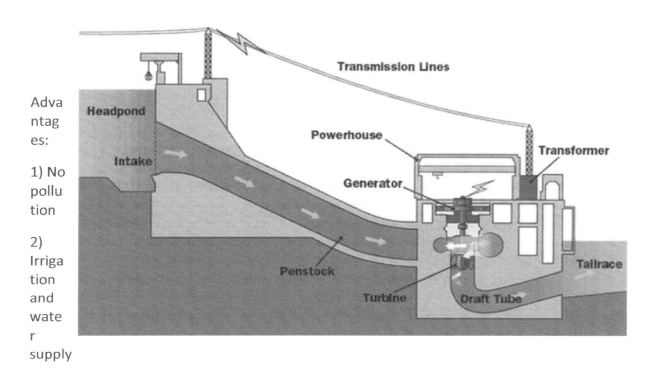

Adva
ntag
es:

1) No
pollu
tion

2)
Irriga
tion
and
wate
r
supply

3) Flood control

4) recreation such as fishing and boating

40. VIADUCT BRIDGE

Viaduct bridge: A type of bridge supported by series of arches

- ➢ It is used to carry road or railway over water or valley or another road
- ➢ This bridge composed of several small spans

41. BUILDING BYE - LAWS

Bye law: The rules are regulations made by town planning authorities regarding requirements of building ensuring safety of public through setbacks, minimum size of rooms, height and number of storey's etc. is called building bye laws.

NOTE: In the view of bhuj earthquake occurred in 2001, the ministry of urban development prepared model building bye-laws in 2003 to ensure structural safety for buildings.

Need of bye laws:

> Provisions of bye laws are safe against fire, noise and structure failure

> To ensure safety and health of people

> Due to these bye laws each building will have proper ventilation

Dwelling: A building or a portion for a family residential

Building bye - laws:

❖ Minimum plot size not < 30 sq. metres

❖ Minimum area of habitable room is 9.5 sq. metres (min. width of room is 2.4 m.)
❖ Minimum plot size of hostel, guesthouse, lodge is 500 sq. metres

❖ Plinth height should not less than 450 mm.

❖ Height of room should not < 2.75 m.

❖ Minimum plot size of dharmashala is 1000 sq. metres and maximum height is 26m.
❖ Chimneys should build at least 0.9 m above flat roofs top of chimney is not below the top of parapet wall. In pitched roofs chimney top shall not < 0.6 m. above ridge of roof.
❖ Parapet walls and hand rails are provided on edges of roof terraces, balcony, verandah etc. Shall not < 1.0 m. and not > 1.2 m.

Motel: A road side hotel having rooms and parking space outside for motor vehicles

❖ minimum plot size is 1 hectare and set back in front is 15 m. Rear and sides is   9 m. And maximum height of motel is 9 m.

Septic tank requirements:

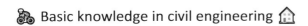

- ❖ It should not closer than 18 m. from well to mitigate bacterial pollution of subsurface water and not closer than 6 m. to building to avoid damage to structure.

- ❖ It shall have minimum width of 750 mm, and minimum depth of 1 m below water level.

- ❖ Minimum liquid capacity is $1m^3$ and minimum nominal diameter of pipe is 0.1m

- ❖ Ventilating pipe of diameter 50 mm with mosquito proof wire mesh.

Stair case requirements: As per NBC 2005 (part 4)

Minimum width of staircase for different buildings

Residential buildings (dwellings) NOTE - For row type house with two storey width shall be 0.75 m	1.0 m
Residential hotel buildings	1.5 m
Assembly buildings like auditorium, theatres, temple etc.	2.0 m
Educational buildings	1.5 m
Institutional buildings	2.0 m

Minimum width of tread: For residential buildings - 250 mm.

For other buildings - 300 mm.

Maximum height of riser: For residential buildings - 190 mm.

For other buildings - 150 mm.

Exit requirements: As per part 4 "Fire and safety" of NBC 2005.

Fire escapes: 1) Fire escape should be constructed of non - combustible materials

2) Fire escape stairs shall have straight flight not less than 125 cm wide with 25 cm treads and risers not > 19 cm.

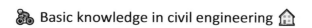 Basic knowledge in civil engineering 🏠

3) Hand rails shall be 100 cm.

4) Fire alarm systems should be provided.

Spiral stairs:

❖ Spiral staircase shall not less than 150 cm of diameter

Ramps:

❖ Ramp width for one-way traffic is 4m and for two-way traffic is 7.2m wide.

❖ Gradient for cars and bikes is 1:10 and for heavy vehicles is 1:15 and at the curved portions the gradient shall not more than 1:12.

❖ The minimum width of ramp in hospitals is 2.4m for stretcher movement.

❖ Ramp shall have a non - slip surface with good material.

Corridor:

Minimum width for passage way / corridors

❖ Residential buildings - dwelling type	=	1.00 m.
❖ Residential building - hostels etc.	=	1.25 m.
❖ Assembly buildings.	=	2.00 m.
❖ Hospitals, nursing homes, etc.	=	2.40 m.
❖ All other buildings including hotels.	=	1.50 m.

Lifts: All floors should be accessible for 24 hours by lifts and for high rise buildings collapsible gates are not permitted solid doors are preferred with fire resistance.

➢ Lifts should have capacity of 545 kg for carrying 8 persons and automated doors are provided.

➢ Alternate power supply shall be provided in all the lifts.

Provision of exterior open spaces around buildings:

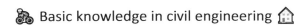 Basic knowledge in civil engineering 🏠

Height of building (m)	Setbacks front rear and sides (m)
10	3
15	5
18	6
21	7
24	8
27	9
30	10
35	11
40	12
45	13
50	14
55 and above	16

Building height in residential premises:

Plot area (sqm)	Maximum height (m)
30	8
30 - 50	8
50 - 100	12
100 - 250	12
250 - 500	15
500 - 1000	15
1000 - 1500	15

For plots up to 4000 sq.mt. The maximum height of building 15 m.

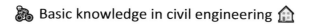 Basic knowledge in civil engineering 🏠

For the plots above 4000 sq.mt. The maximum height of building is 26m.

All the buildings having plot size of 100 sqm. or more while submitting the building plans for sanction, shall mandatorily include complete proposal of rainwater harvesting.

Rain water can be harvested about 55,000 litres per 100 sqm. area per year from roof tops.

Water requirement for various occupancies: consumption per head per day (in lt.)

In Residential: 1) In living units and hostels - 135 lit per head per day

2) Hotels (with lodging accommodation per bed) - 180 lit.

3) Hotels (5 star) - 340 lit.

In Educational: 1) Day schools - 45 lit.

In cinema theatres, auditorium per seat - 15 litres.

Toilet facilities in public places: 1) flushing urinals - 0.2 lit.

2) Toilet including washing hands - 7 lit.

In Hospitals: 1) beds up to 100 is 340 lit.

2) beds greater than 100 is 450 lit.

42. CRACKS

Crack: A line created on the surface of something which is split without breaking apart or a gap formed on surface.

Cracks may form in structures due to many reasons like faulty materials, faulty construction, improper workmanship, environmental factors etc.

> In some sites the soil like black cotton having expanding properties in moisture conditions and when dry conditions occur it shrinks, this causes movement in foundations and results in cracks in building.

Shrinkage: Reduction in volume.
Shrinkage causes cracks in rcc structure

1) plastic shrinkage: It occurs very soon after pouring concrete in forms due to evaporation from surface and leads to cracks.

2) Dry shrinkage: After setting and hardening of concrete due to loss of capillary water it causes shrinkage

3) carbonation shrinkage: Due to the reaction of carbon dioxide with calcium hydroxide in cement results in calcium carbonate.

4) Autogenous shrinkage: Due to no moisture movement from concrete paste it resulting this type of shrinkage

It occurs in dams due to no moisture movement.

43. VAASTU

Vaastu: The term "Vaastu" is a Sanskrit word which means place to live

Vaastu is first mentioned in Yajurveda which is holy book of Hindus

Vaastu is preferred for all buildings for the purpose of living happily, peaceful, and healthy life.

Our entire universe is made of five basic elements they are water, air, earth, fire, space. These are called as "pancha mahabhootas".

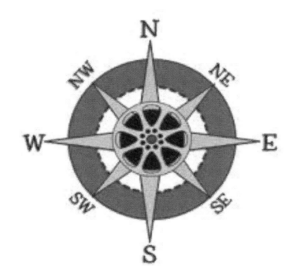

All these five elements should be in equilibrium which results in prosperity, health etc.

Our human body is also having five sense organs, they are ear, nose, tongue, eye, skin.

According to Vedas: 1) North East is ruled by lord Shiva

                    2) south is ruled by Yama

By all this we understand that positive and negative energy flow in to the house

So, we should obstruct negative energy and allow positive energy in to the house.

Some of the Vaastu principles while constructing building are:

❖ Main door of building should be provided in East, North or North - East.

❖ Site should be in rectangle or square.

❖ Slope should be provided towards North - East and higher level is kept at south west.

❖ Bore well shall be preferred in North - East of building.

❖ Balcony is preferred in North and East.

❖ Verandah shall be preferred in north and east for sit out and relax and get vitamin-D from sun light daily morning.

❖ Hall is preferred in North - East, South - West, West, East.

❖ Kitchen shall be located in south - east and north - west.

❖ Bedroom is preferred in south - west, west but avoid in north east and south east.

❖ Pooja room should be located in North - East.

❖ Bathroom is preferred in East and North.

❖ Toilet shall prefer in North - west and west.

❖ Staircase should be provided in south or south - west to obstruct negative energy entering in to house.

❖ Proper ventilation should be there in building to get air circulation

❖ Open area shall be preferred in North

❖ South side is not preferred to have open space, for avoiding negative energy there should be heavy mass, so for that staircase is preferred in that location.

Out of all these principles I conclude that to get positive energy flow inside the house North side of house should be open and south side should be closed completely or partially depending upon road in front of building is at which direction.

  ➢ South direction is preferred in facing head while sleeping to avoid bad dreams.

These principles should be followed for leading happy, health, and peaceful life.

🚲 Basic knowledge in civil engineering 🏠

44. MILE STONE

Mile stone: A stone placed beside road having numbered distance in miles or kilometres to a particular place.

For travellers to know how much distance is there to certain place

> ➢ For national highway it is in yellow and the white colour.
>
> ➢ For state highway it is in green and white colour.
>
> ➢ For district roads it is in black and white colour.
>
> ➢ For village roads it is in orange and white colour.

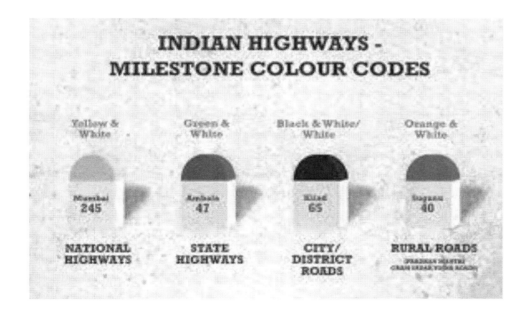

45. CLIMATE AND WEATHER

Climate: It is an atmospheric condition prevailing in an area over a long period of time.

If Summer is hotter, we say recent climate is hot

Weather: It is condition for short period of time i.e. hour to hour, day to day changes in clouds, wind, temperature.

46. COLUMN MARKING

Column marking layout is done and executed in field by marking on site with lime powder.

3-4-5 rule is made while marking in field.

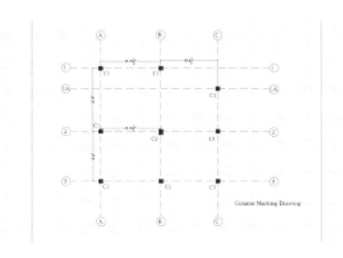

Column Marking Drawing

47. CLADDING

Cladding: cladding is a covering material applied over another as a layer.

Advantages of cladding in buildings:

1) Improve appearance of building.

2) For thermal insulation.

3) Weather resistance.

➢ Now-a-days cladding is using for all buildings for aesthetic appearance.

It is made up of many materials such as wood, metal, brick, aluminium, fibres etc.

Aluminium composite panels are using in construction elevations

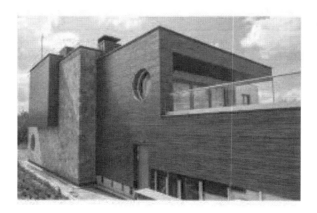

48. How to calculate cement, fine aggregate, coarse aggregate and water required for plain cement concrete member

Consider a plain cement concrete member.

Size of member = 4.0 × 18 × 0.12 m.

Volume = 8.64 cubic. Meters.

But volume of dry concrete is 1.54 times the wet concrete

Then dry volume = 8.64×1.54 = 13.31 m^3.

Grade of concrete is M20 = 1:1.5:3.

So, 1+1.5+3 = 5.5.

★ **Cement calculation:** 1×13.31/5.5 = 2.42m^3.

= 2.42×1440 = 3484 kgs.   (density of cement = 1440 kg/m^3.)

Cement bags = 3484/50 = 70 no's.   (1cement bag = 50 kg)

★ **Fine aggregate calculation:**

= 1.5×13.31/5.5 = 3.63 m^3.

= 3.63×1600 = 5808 kg.   (Density of sand is 1600kg/m^3.)

= 5.808 ~= 6 tonnes   (1 tonne = 1000kg.)

★ **Coarse aggregate calculation:**

= 3×13.31/5.5 = 7.26 m^3.

= 7.26×1560 = 11325.6 kg.   (Density of C.A = 1560 kg/m^3.)

= 11.33 tonnes.

🚲 Basic knowledge in civil engineering 🏠

★ **Water calculation:**

      = 3484×0.5 = 1742 kg   (w/c = 0.5)

      = 1742 lit.

49.WATER

Water is the main ingredient for hydration of cement

- ➤ It plays main role in increasing strength of concrete.
- ➤ If the W/C is less than 0.45 then concrete is not workable and leads to honey combed structure containing large number of voids.

- ➤ If more water is used in mix causes bleeding and segregation.
- ➤ Curing is done for 28 days to get almost full strength.
- ➤ Water should be free from salts, organic matter, oils, alkalies etc.
- ➤ PH of water should not less than 6 for water used in construction.

Permissible limits of impurities in water:

Impurity	As per	Permissible limit (max)
Organic	IS 3025 (part 18)	200 mg/l.
Inorganic	IS 3025 (part 18)	3000 mg/l.
Sulphates	IS 3025 (part 24)	400 mg/l.
Chlorides	IS 3025 (part 32)	2000 mg/l. for p.c.c. and 500 mg/l. for R.C.C.
Suspended matter	IS 3025 (part 17)	2000 mg/l.

50. GALVANIZED IRON

Galvanization: It is a process of coating iron or steel with protective layer of zinc.

➢ To prevent rusting of iron.

➢ Common method used is "Hot dip galvanizing" in this the iron parts are submerged in molten zinc material.

G.I sheets are using as roofing material and G.I pipes are also using to prevent corrosion.

G.I iron sheets

Aluminium - zinc alloy colour coated steel sheets; these sheets are invented to make more resistant against corrosion. This sheet is 2 to 4 times much corrosion resistant than G.I sheet.

51. FORM WORK

Form work: A temporary structure used as mould to pour the concrete and support until it gets hardened and becomes self-supported is called form work

- ➤ Form work is shuttering, centring, props.
- ➤ Form work is made of timber, steel.
- ➤ Form work should have good strength and durability
- ➤ It should be water tight member to prevent leakage.

Shuttering: It is vertical temporary arrangement used as mould for columns, beam sides, slab sides.

Centring: It is a horizontal arrangement used to support slab bottom, beam bottom.

🛵 Basic knowledge in civil engineering 🏠

Props: These are vertical supporting Members for supporting centring.

Props are provided under the centring formwork to carry loads safely.

Props shall be strong to should bear the dead load of concrete.

Scaffolding: It is a temporary structure having platform provided with supports used for workers during building operations.

Stripping of formwork: Forms are removed after the concrete has achieved strength of at least twice the stress to which concrete may be subjected at the time of removal of formwork.

Stripping time as per IS 456 - 2000 when ordinary Portland cement is used are given below.

Type of formwork	Minimum period before striking
Vertical formwork to columns, walls, beams.	16 - 24 hrs.
Soffit form work to slabs (props to be refixed immediately after removal of formwork).	3 days
Soffit form work to beams (props to be refixed immediately after the removal of form work)	7 days
Props to slabs: 1) spanning up to 4.5 m 2) spanning over 4.5 m	 7 days 14 days
Props to beams and arches: 1) spanning up to 6 m. 2) spanning over 6 m.	 14 days 21 days

★ For others cements stripping time may be modified.

★ Soffit means under surface of member.

52. EARTHQUAKE AND ZONES IN INDIA

Earthquake: A sudden violent shaking of ground results in destructive effect.

Causes:

1) Movement of tectonic plates.

2) Volcanic eruptions.

3) Underground nuclear explosions.

Earthquake is recorded by an instrument called "seismograph".

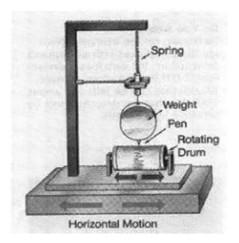

Earthquake zones in India: As per IS: 1893 (part 1) - 2002.

India has been divided into four zones

- ➢ Zone - 2
- ➢ Zone - 3
- ➢ Zone - 4
- ➢ Zone - 5

Out of these zone - 5 is having more seismicity.

Zone - 5: Regions of central Himalayas, Kutch area in Gujarat, Kashmir, north and middle of Bihar.

Zone - 4: Regions of Jammu and Kashmir, Himachal Pradesh, Uttarakhand, Sikkim.

Zone - 3 and zone -2 are remaining.

★ In the fifth revision of IS 1893 (part 1) - 2002. Zone-1 is merged to zone-2
★ So, zone-1 does not appear in new zoning and instead of five zones there are four zones presently.

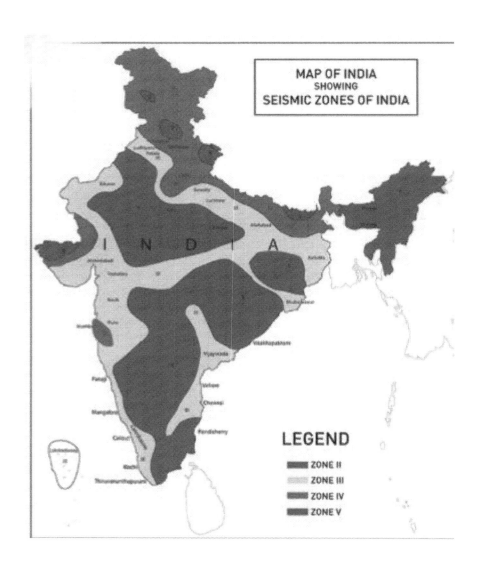

> In India major earthquake has occurred in Gujarat, bhuj in 26th Jan. 2001 with a magnitude of 7.7 killed 15,000 members.
> Earthquake magnitude is determined by Charles Richter's magnitude.

Charles Richter presented Richter scale in 1935.

Richter magnitude	Earthquake effects
Less than 3.5	Generally, not felt but recorded
3.5 - 5.4	Felt and rarely cause damage
5.5 - 6.0	Slight damage to well-designed building and more damage to poorly constructed buildings.
6.1 - 6.9	Can be destructive in areas up to 100 km where people live.
7.0 - 7.9	Major earthquake causing serious damage over large areas.
8 and more	Great earthquake can cause severe damage for about several 100 km in areas

53. RAIN WATER HARVESTING PIT

➤ It is a technique of collection and storage of rain water for many purposes.

➤ Rain water is collected from roof tops and used for ground water recharge because due to rapid urbanization ground water levels are decreasing now a days.

➤ It is used for ground water recharge, for water to gardens etc.

Recharging pits are having 1 to 2m wide and 3m deep.

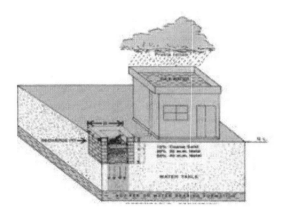

Rain water harvesting and ground water recharge for individual plotted house.

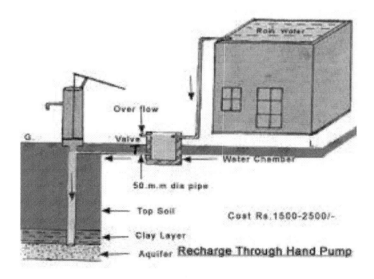

54. QUICK SAND

❖ It is a colloid hydrogel consisting of fine granular material of (sand, silt, clay) and water.

It forms in saturated loose sand when water in sand cannot escape soil loses its strength and can't support weight

It sucks if anything falling on it and mainly formed near coastal areas, lakes etc.

Liquefaction is occurred due to earthquake and in liquefaction soil loss shear strength

55. WATER BODIES (RIVER, STREAM, LAKE, POND, LAGOON, ESTUARY)

River: It is a natural flowing water course usually freshwater which flows finally in to ocean or sea.

➢ River is larger, longer and deeper than stream.
➢ Nile river is the longest river in world with a length of 6650 km.

Stream: It is a flowing water body but not deeper and wider and we can easily walk in stream.

It is a narrow way of water course.

Stream

Lake: It is the area filled with water enclosed by land.

It is a still water body.

lake

 Basic knowledge in civil engineering 🏠

Pond: It is the area filled with water and enclosed by land but it is smaller than lake.

Lagoon: It is the water body formed near coastal areas and it is shallow having small link with sea or ocean separated by island or reefs.

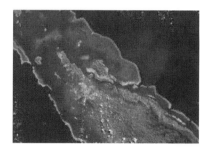

Estuary: It is a place partially enclosed by coastal body of brackish water with one or more rivers and connecting to sea or ocean

It is the place where fresh and salt water meet.

Brackish water means slightly salty water.

56. COVER FOR ENVIRONMENTAL EXPOSURE CONDITIONS

As per IS: 456-2000 exposure conditions are given for providing cover to reinforcement depending upon site conditions

Environment	Exposure conditions
Mild	Concrete surfaces protected against weather conditions except those in coastal areas.
Moderate	Concrete exposed to rain and concrete is contact with ground water but sheltered from saturated salt air in coastal area.
Severe	Concrete surface exposed to severe rain alternate wetting and drying or occasional freezing and exposed to coastal area and concrete immersed in sea water.
Very severe	Concrete is exposed to sea water and corrosive fumes and severe freezing. And contact with aggressive sub-soil
Extreme	Surface members in tidal zone and where contact with liquid or solid aggressive chemicals.

Nominal cover for exposure conditions:

Exposure	Nominal cover not less than
Mild	20
Moderate	30
Severe	45
Very severe	50
Extreme	75

57. EPOXY INJECTION

Epoxy resin or an adhesive containing artificial substance used for repairing cracks with grout inject.

Procedure:

- ➤ Drill the crack from the concrete face.
- ➤ Inject water to flush out defect
- ➤ Allow surface to dry
- ➤ Making the holes of 3/4 inch diameter then pipes are fixed along crack
- ➤ Epoxy is injected through holes of pipe.

58. DETAILED AND ABSTRACT ESTIMATE

Estimation is the process of calculating quantities and cost of various items.

Detailed estimation: In this estimate the quantities of each item of work such as earth work excavation, brick masonry, RCC slab etc.

The proforma is given below:

Item No.	Description of Item	No's	Length	Breadth	Depth	Quantity	Total Quantity

For getting administrative approval, approximate estimate is prepared.

For getting technical sanction, detailed estimate is prepared.

Abstract estimate: This gives exact cost of project

Proforma of abstract estimate:

Item No.	Quantity	Description of Item	Rate	Per	Amount

59. BAR BENDING SCHEDULE

For estimation of total quantity of steel bar bending schedule is prepared

DESCRIPTION OF ITEM	DIA OF BAR	SHAPE OF BAR	LENGTH IN (M).	NO'S.	TOTAL LENGTH (M).	WEIGHT IN KG/M.	TOTAL WEIGHT IN KG.

Some technical points:

➢ Minimum diameter of longitudinal bar in column is 12 mm.

➢ Minimum diameter of stirrups and lateral ties is 6 mm.

➢ Minimum diameter of dowel bar is 12 mm. (Dowel bar is used in footing for proper transfer of load).

➢ Minimum diameter of bar in slab is 8 mm.

➢ Maximum diameter of bar in slab shall not exceed the 1/8 of total thickness of slab.

➢ Minimum number of bars in rectangular column is 4 no's. And for circular column is 6 no's.

MY CONCEPT

In my point of view if you want to improve your knowledge you should involve in doing something by practical application.

It makes you

- ➤ Thick innovatively.
- ➤ You can get new ideas and new formulas for a particular problem.
- ➤ It improves your skill.

Don't read books blindly.

You should think up your mind to get new ideas to achieve something

- ★ To achieve your goals, you must have interest and patience.

Do the work what your mind tells.

Many obstacles come in life you have to overcome them to reach success.

Success or failure is doesn't matter but your experience is important

For example, I have written a small book even though it is good or average doesn't matter but the experience in writing the book is important.

Here experience is knowledge.

Respect others

Respect yourself

Respect your profession.

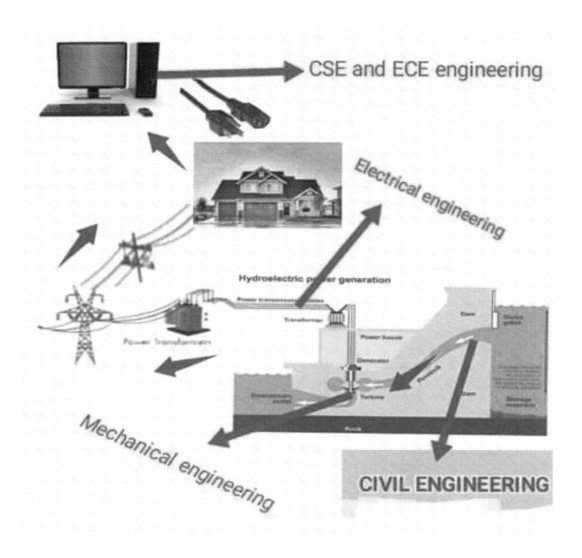

This is civil engineering

Civil engineering

Most important in our daily life

❖ *For living we need a shelter*

❖ *For transportation we need roads and railway tracks*

❖ *To cross a river or valley we need bridge*

My life towards writing –

When I was 19, I was a student of Bachelor of technology in civil engineering third year, I wrote this book at that time.

Our brain will remember the things more precisely, which we have seen it with our naked eye, rather than we imagined it.

Therefore, to avoid this problem, pictures and diagrams are given to the particular topic, which makes easily understand and remember. This book really helps some students who began their journey towards civil engineering.

Actually, I'm an Indian, so this book seems more relevant to India. But more than 75% content is useful for everyone, not only Indian.

My second book which is _Non-Fictitious – Fiction Book = P+P: (JOURNEY OF A BOY)_

My third book is Basic knowledge in civil engineering part 2: Book of 49 topics which is perspicuous one. Part 2 book is written with some home-based simple experiments which helps a lot to student and also having good ratings and review. If you buy this part 2 book you 'll definitely feel more than pleased, and you say it as best book.

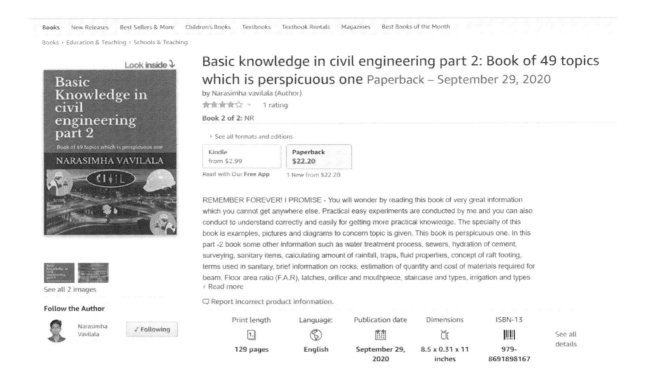

Books   New Releases   Best Sellers & More   Children's Books   Textbooks   Textbook Rentals   Magazines   Best Books of the Month

Books › Education & Teaching › Schools & Teaching

Basic knowledge in civil engineering part 2: Book of 49 topics which is perspicuous one Paperback – September 29, 2020

by Narasimha vavilala (Author)

★★★★☆ ˅   1 rating

Book 2 of 2: NR

› See all formats and editions

Kindle from $2.99	Paperback $22.20
Read with Our Free App	1 New from $22.20

REMEMBER FOREVER! I PROMISE - You will wonder by reading this book of very great information which you cannot get anywhere else. Practical easy experiments are conducted by me and you can also conduct to understand correctly and easily for getting more practical knowledge. The specialty of this book is examples, pictures and diagrams to concern topic is given. This book is perspicuous one. In this part -2 book some other information such as water treatment process, sewers, hydration of cement, surveying, sanitary items, calculating amount of rainfall, traps, fluid properties, concept of raft footing, terms used in sanitary, brief information on rocks, estimation of quantity and cost of materials required for beam, Floor area ratio (F.A.R), latches, orifice and mouthpiece, staircase and types, irrigation and types ‹ Read more

⬚ Report incorrect product information.

Print length	Language:	Publication date	Dimensions	ISBN-13	See all details
129 pages	English	September 29, 2020	8.5 x 0.31 x 11 inches	979-8691898167	

This is special distinct book. Practical experiments conducted by me for easy understanding extremely useful book than part one.

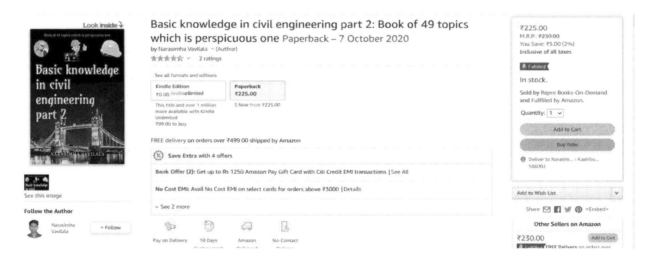

Some of the topics in the part 2 book are in next page.

 Basic knowledge in civil engineering 🏠

SURFACE TENSION

It is the property of a liquid surface that resist an external force. It is expressed in N/m.

Before knowing about surface tension, you have to know about the adhesion and cohesion.

Adhesion: It is the property of liquid which sticks to another surface.

Examples:

1) Water having more adhesion which you can observe by conducting a simple experiment i.e., Take one of your finger and dip in water, then take out your finger and come close it to your other hand finger, then you can notice the attraction like a magnet by water molecule and cling to your finger surface, which is called adhesion.

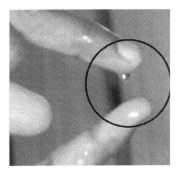 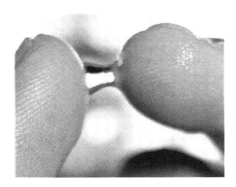

Without adhesion, water don't lie between your fingers & won't stick, it just falls down.

Cohesion: It is the attraction between molecules of liquid, which sticks together and form a whole.

Water is a molecule, but when you add it to other water molecule it becomes whole.

Examples:

1) Without cohesion, water in a beaker appears in the form of rain in flight; like droplets.

2) You can clearly observe cohesion also by the finger test with a droplet, just like first example of adhesion experiment given above. This time, dip both fingers in water (molecules attach to both fingers), then Make fingers come closer to each other. It attaches and form whole one.

slowly separate your fingers from each other, you can also observe the cohesion between particles making the whole droplet like an elastic material.

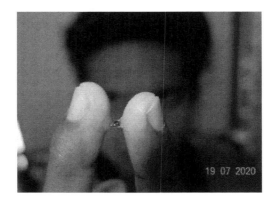

Cohesion between water molecules; it's a bond.

Surface tension: Surface tension occurs due to the cohesive forces between molecules of the liquid. The cohesive forces pull inward and behave like a whole one which resist an external force.

IMPORTANT TOPICS WITH PRACTICAL EXPERIMENTS, I WRITTEN IN THIS BOOK.

1) Placed slowly   2) Dropped simply

1) In the above picture, I placed a steel sheet on water slowly & gently, without applying much force, it floated. Actually, steel having more density than water, but here why it doesn't sink, this is happened due to surface tension, which only resist certain capable force, if force exceeds than its resistance, it results the second one. (Note: steel sheet should be dry while placing)

2) If you simply drop the steel sheet, it breaks the cohesion between molecules and leads sinking to the bottom.

Thank you

Printed in Great Britain
by Amazon

32133403R00053